BoyCraft

Loads of things to make
FOR and WITH boys (and girls)

Frances Lincoln Ltd
74–77 White Lion Street
London N1 9PF
www.franceslincoln.com

BoyCraft
Copyright © Frances Lincoln Limited 2014
Text copyright © Sara Duchars and Sarah Marks 2014
Illustrations copyright © Nicola Kent 2014
Photographs copyright © Dan Duchars 2014
First Frances Lincoln edition 2014

British Library Cataloguing-in-Publication data
A catalogue record for this book is available from the British Library.

ISBN: 978-0-7112-3489-5

Printed and bound in China

9 8 7 6 5 4 3 2 1

BOY CRAFT

Loads of things to make FOR and WITH boys (and girls)

SARA DUCHARS & SARAH MARKS

Illustrations by Nicola Kent

buttonbag

F
FRANCES LINCOLN LIMITED
PUBLISHERS

Projects

PAPER CRAFT

STITCH CRAFT

Big enough to get all your kit in

Lots of the sewing projects are recrafted from old clothes and other household textiles. It's a great way to breathe new life into things you might be about to throw away

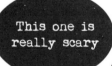

This one is really scary

CREEPY CRAFT

WOOD CRAFT

You can make things out of wood without needing lots of tools - try making some stick insects with twigs and string

MODEL CRAFT

WOOLLY CRAFT

Why BoyCraft?

Between the two of us we have three boys and a tomboy, aged between eight and twelve, so our houses have been full of boys playing, shouting, making, breaking and creating – mostly chaos but the occasional masterpiece – for well over a decade. There are plenty of craft books out there for girls but even the ones that don't have pink frilly cupcakes on the cover are often full of handbags, fairy wings and princess tiaras. We wanted to create a craft book full of projects that would appeal to boys and tomboys everywhere. We wanted to include all the kinds of crafty things that boys love doing before they get the idea that craft isn't boy-ish enough. So although *BoyCraft* has both sewing and knitting projects, it has also got lots of woodwork and modelmaking, and even projects for action men. *BoyCraft* is not anti-girls (there are a fair number of girls dotted thoughout these pages) but we have deliberately left out the pink frilly bits.

Kids have been making toys out of the junk that adults throw away for years – go-karts from broken prams, trains from old boxes or soldiers and other figures from traditional wooden pegs. What has changed however, is the kind of junk being used. Many of the the projects in this book reflect the contents of today's recycling bin: lots of plastic milk bottles and lids, yoghurt pots, plastic drinking bottles, acrylic jumpers, old t-shirts, plastic bags, CDs and other modern-life detritus. Our earlier book *ReCraft* was all about turning old things into new. *BoyCraft* continues that tradition. This book includes projects for adults to make for the boys in their life. It's also for all kids who love making things, but particularly the boys who don't yet know they love making stuff. We hope, after trying some of the projects in this book, they will.

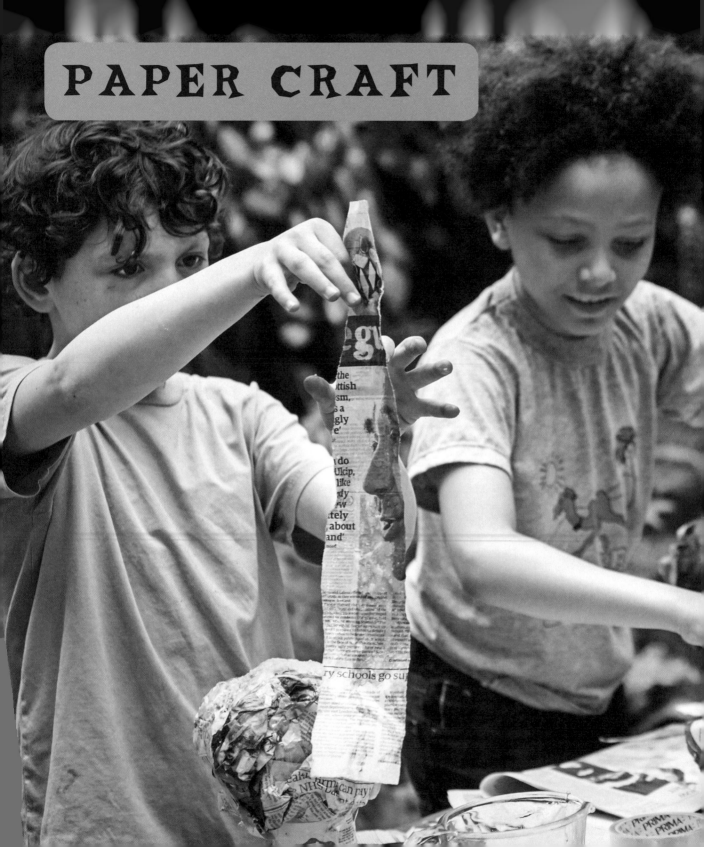

PAPER CRAFT

Papier mache
p.11

Fun with paper

Ever since the ancient Egyptians discovered that inking hieroglyphics on to a piece of pulped-up, dried-out papyrus was easier than carving them into a block of stone people have been having fun with paper. The Japanese even created a whole art out of it – origami. Although, anyone who's ever tried to fold a jumping frog or a farting elephant will know it's a lot harder than it looks! But have patience young crafter, a few simple origami-style folds can transform a plain piece of paper into a fiendish water bomb – what could be more fun than that? See page 22 for the full details.

The paper lying around your home is the basis for lots of great projects – from paper sculpture heads, to bowls, fantasy landscapes and good old fashioned paper chains (old comics work particularly well here).

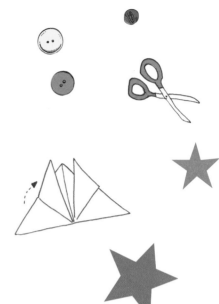

How to: Papier mache

You can make all kinds of things with papier mache, using just paper and glue or starch. Both PVA glue or wallpaper paste work well. Wallpaper paste is loads of fun to make. It's like magic cold porridge but can take up to a week to dry so we prefer using PVA glue. Beware – this is messy! Cover the table with a plastic cloth or bin bags or better still, do it outside. Have a large bucket of soapy water nearby so you can rinse off your hands when they get too sticky.

Mix glue and water in a big bowl or a saucepan. A good mix for PVA papier mache is about one part glue to about three parts water.
If using wallpaper paste, make it so that the consistency is thicker than the instructions on the pack.
Before you begin, tear up lots of newspaper into strips ready to use. You'll find that paper rips much more easily in one direction than the other. Don't make the strips too wide or too long.
Use the strips of paper dipped in your PVA glue mix or wallpaper paste to cover an object or create your own shape. Let it dry and then paint and decorate!

Papier mache heads

You will need

- Large yoghurt pot
- Sticky tape
- Newspaper
- PVA glue
- Paint, pens and other things for decorating

This is a quick and easy way to make quite big paper heads. It's much less complicated than using a balloon and it's a great project for Halloween – see evil heads on page 66. Ordinary PVA glue dries much faster than wallpaper paste – but either is fun.

1. Make a big ball by first rolling up newspaper and tying it in a knot. Add other newspaper tubes, tucking in the ends as you go. Continue until it's about the size of a large grapefruit, using tape to hold it in shape. Don't worry if it's wonky – that's part of the fun.

2. Tape the paper ball to the bottom of the upturned yoghurt pot. Dilute some PVA with water in a bowl (about 1 part glue to 3 parts water). Tear newspaper into strips, dip into the glue mix and begin to cover the head and yoghurt pot, until it is completely covered.

3. Create features by moulding newspaper and attaching firmly with additional glue strips. Continue until all the features are in place and the surface is fairly smooth. Leave until completely dry – overnight for PVA papier mache but up to a week with wallpaper paste!

4. To decorate, paint with household emulsion or poster paint. Either paint or draw on features with a marker pen or thick felt-tips. Glue on wool for hair or make some from fabric scraps – fake fur or fleece is ideal. Use plenty of PVA or a strong craft glue.

Use a small
scrunched up ball of
newspaper for a nose

and a twisted strip
for eyes or a mouth

plastic bag

Sponge

JUICE CARTON

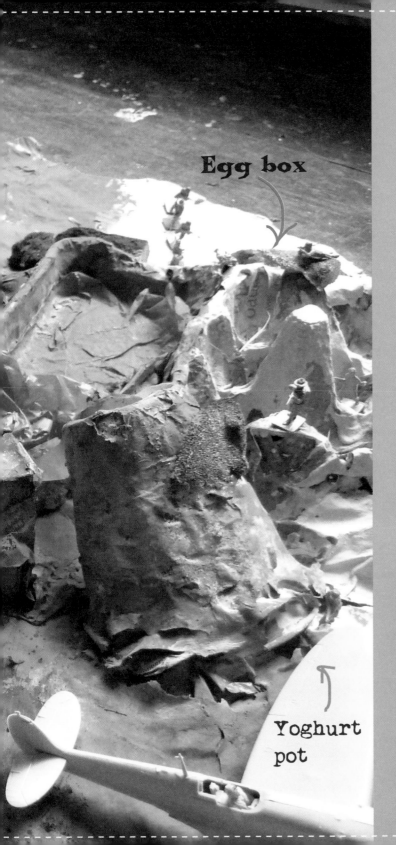

Egg box

Yoghurt pot

Landscapes

These papier mache bases are great for creating fantasy lanscapes for toy soldiers, Warhammer figures and other small toys. Invite some friends round and make a giant one by butting up additional bases.

Cut a base from some sturdy cardboard. Tape a variety of small boxes and cardboard tubes to it. Cover the entire surface with papier mache (see page 11) and leave to dry. Paint with poster paint or household emulsion and add any details. Chopped up sponge makes good bushes and foliage and strips of blue plastic bag can be glued on to create rivers. When paint is dry you can add more details with felt tip pens.

Magazine bowls

You will need
- Old magazines
- Sticky tape
- Clothes pegs
- PVA glue

Make these easy bowls and pencil holders from pages of magazines.

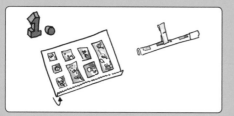

1. Tear out a page from the magazine. Starting from the torn edge, fold it up into a long strip about 1cm (½in) wide. Hold in place with a peg or place under a heavy book. Continue to fold more pages in the same way, until you have used up about half the magazine.

2. Take one of your strips, fold over one end and then start rolling the strip into a spiral. When you reach the end, hold it firmly while you attach another strip to it with sticky tape. Keep going in this way until you have a flat spiral about 10cm (4in) in diameter.

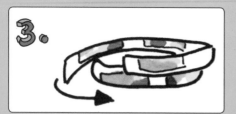

3. Now place your next strip about half way up the side of the previous one and carry on winding it around. Secure the end with tape and stick on another strip. Keep going, gradually moving up the bowl as you are building up the sides.

4. When you have made the bowl big enough make sure the end is securely taped. Then paint the inside with a mixture of equal parts PVA glue and water. When this is completely dry, turn the bowl over and paint the glue mixture on the underside. You might want to repeat these steps and give it several more coats of glue.

Experiment with different sizes and shapes of bowls and pots.

Medals for bravery

Use the templates on page 118 to create medals from thin card. These shapes are based on real historical medals. Some of them, like the Victoria Cross and the George Cross, are still awarded for acts of extreme valour. You can create an embossed effect by tracing the design with biro on the reverse so the design shows through on the front (see below) or you can make up your own design. Thread a short piece of wide ribbon through the slot and use a safety pin to fix in place.

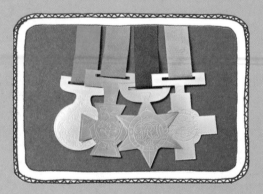

Paper chains

Ever wondered what to do with all your old *Beanos* – or other comics – once you've read them hundreds of times and they are falling apart? Try turning them into an old-fashioned paper chain – it's a brilliant way of decorating your home for Christmas or a party. Cut up the middle of the comic and then cut each page into strips about 2cm (¾in) wide. Staple or tape the ends of the first piece together to create a circle, put the next piece through and join the ends to make the next link in the chain. Now just keep going until you've had enough. (This is how people decorated their homes before tinsel was invented!)

Water bombs

You don't have to fill these with water and throw them at your friends – you can string them up and use them as decorations.

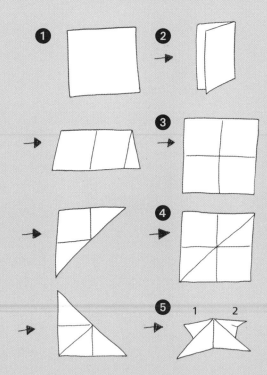

1. Start with a square of paper (a page from a comic is fine).
2. Fold the paper in half and then in half again.
3. Open back out and fold corner to corner.
4. Open up again and fold the other corner to corner.
5. Open back out and start folding it along folds 1 and 2 at the same time. It looks a bit like a collapsing pyramid at this stage. You should end up with a flat triangle.

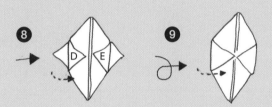

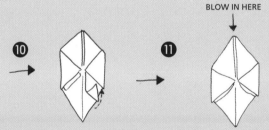

BLOW IN HERE

THIS IS THE HOLE TO POUR WATER IN

6. Fold point A and B up towards C.

7. Turn over and do the same to the other side. It should look like a diamond with a vertical line down the middle.

8. Fold D and E in to the middle.

9. Turn over and do the same to the other side.

10. Fold the two points at the bottom into the flaps. Turn over and do the same to the other side.

11. Gently blow into the hole at the top to inflate into a cube shape.

Fill with water and throw!

STITCH CRAFT

Jumper monkeys
p.30

How to: Sew

Sewing has traditionally been a man's job and there's nothing girly about working with razor sharp scissors, shears and needles. A needle might be a lot smaller than a sword but it's still got a sharp end and there's something magical about the way this small piece of metal and a little bit of thread can transform flat pieces of fabric into something three-dimensional. Sewing machines are really cool too. Using the foot control pedal is a lot like learning to drive a car. You have to press down just hard enough or it races away out of control. The small bean bags on page 38 are a good starter project for machine-sewing novices. You can't really go wrong – even if they don't turn out as perfect squares you can still juggle with them. The jumper monkeys on page 30 are also surprisingly easy to make. Don't bother buying lots of expensive fabric. Old clothes, including t-shirts, sweatshirts and jeans are great for practising your sewing skills, however fleece is worth splashing out on as it is easy to cut, sew and doesn't fray. It comes in lots of bright colours (see the gadget cases on page 48 and the hats on page 42) and patterns too. We used a tiger stripe for the giant bean bag on pages 36–7.

Tool kit

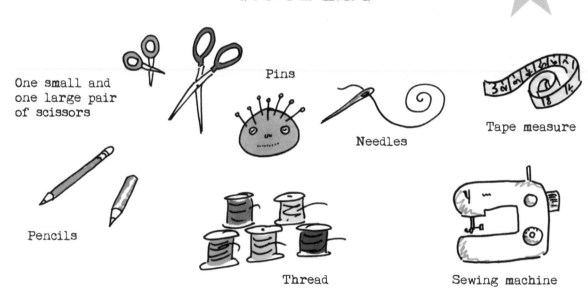

One small and one large pair of scissors

Pins

Needles

Tape measure

Pencils

Thread

Sewing machine

Stitches

Start all stitching by threading your needle with about 40cm (16in) of thread and tie a knot in the end to stop the thread from going all the way through your fabric. When you run out of thread or have finished your line of stitching, do two or three stitches on the same spot to stop your thread unravelling.

RUNNING STITCH

This is the simplest stitch and the one you will probably use the most. Push the needle from the underside of the fabric to the top. Gently pull the thread tight. Push the needle back through the fabric from top to bottom about 5mm along, but instead of pushing all the way through, poke tip back through to top of fabric about 5mm along. Push through from the top. So although the needle and thread goes from top to bottom to make each stitch, you are always going to pull (or push) the needle through from the top. This makes it easier to get a straight line and even-sized stitches.

GATHERING STITCH

This is a running stitch but using longer stitches, which are then pulled tight to gather the fabric up. The bigger the stitches, the bigger the gathers.

OVER AND OVER STITCH

Basically you sew over and over the edge of the fabric. This is great for sewing patches onto your jeans or your name on to a bag. Push the needle from the underside of the fabric to the top, about 5mm from the edge, or more if you want your stitches to be bigger. Pull the thread tight, take it over the edge of the fabric and push the needle back in from the underside of the fabric about 5mm along.

BLANKET STITCH

A slightly trickier version of over and over stitch traditionally used for the edges of woollen blankets. It can be used when you want a more decorative edge. Push the needle in about 5mm away from the edge of the fabric and, holding the thread along the edge of the fabric, bring it out again, making sure the thread is behind the needle. Pull tight and repeat.

BACK STITCH

This is a very useful stitch when you need a very strong line of stitches that aren't going to rip easily. Start with a running stitch, then bring the needle up again, the same distance away from the end of the stitch. Now do a back stitch – take the needle back down at the end of the first stitch. Repeat.

Techniques

SEWING A SEAM
A seam will hold two pieces of fabric together. Lay one piece on top of the other with the right sides of the fabric on the inside. Put a couple of pins through to hold them in place, then either sew a running stitch by hand or machine sew a line about 1.5cm (½in) from the edge. Press the seam open with an iron after sewing.

SEWING A HEM
This is what you do at the bottom of a piece of fabric to stop it fraying. Turn up 1.5cm (½in), press with an iron, then fold over again and press. Machine or hand sew a running stitch all the way along.

NOTCHING
Sometimes you might want to turn a curved seam through to the other side, for example if you are making one of the jumper monkeys on page 30. The seam will only lie flat if you carefully cut a few triangular bits out of the fabric before turning through. These are called notches. Be very careful not to cut through your stitches!

THREADING A CORD THROUGH A CHANNEL
This is very useful for projects such as the denim duffel bag on page 44. Fold over enough fabric to make a channel or fabric 'tunnel' for your cord or whatever it is you want to thread through. Machine sew it down, leaving enough of a gap to get a big safety pin through. Attach the safety pin to one end of the cord then push it into the channel, and gradually push it all the way round, pulling the cord behind it. Make sure you don't let the other end disappear in the channel.

MAKING A PLEAT
A pleat is a fold in the fabric and is often used to make something look fuller or more three-dimensional. You can fold the fabric over to the side, then stitch it down, or fold two sides in to the middle before sewing across the top to hold in place.

APPLIQUE
Use this technique to sew a patch on the hole in your jeans, sew your name on your PE bag, or your favourite band's name on your t-shirt. The best fabrics to use are those which don't fray, such as felt or t-shirt fabric. Cut out your shape, position and stick on with fabric glue, or use a running stitch or over and over stitch to secure it in place.

STUFFING
You can buy toy stuffing from any good haberdashery, or you can cut up old t-shirts or socks into very small pieces. Finish your sewing leaving a small opening and carefully push the stuffing in through this hole. Use a blunt pencil to push it into the corners. For the mini bean bags on page 38 we used rice and dried beans for the stuffing and for the giant bean bags we used polystyrene balls which you can buy from a haberdashery or from our website (www.buttonbag.co.uk).

Jumper monkeys

You will need

- Old jumper
- Buttons and fabric scraps to make the face
- Stuffing
- Basic sewing kit
- Sewing machine
- Velcro to add to the hands so your monkey can hug you (optional)

Turn old jumpers into cuddly monkeys and apes. The basic pattern can be easily adaped to make orangutans, chimps, and all kinds of unique monkey creations. These can be hand or machine sewn.

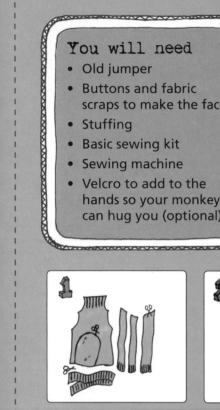

Turn the jumper inside out and lay it flat on a table. Cut off the sleeves and cut both in half down the length. These will become the legs and arms. With a pencil or chalk draw a big arched shape with a flat bottom on the main part of the jumper. This will be your monkey's body. Pin through both sides of the jumper and cut out about 2cm (¾in) outside the line you have drawn. Cut as long a strip as possible from the bottom of the jumper for the tail, and two ear shapes from scraps.

Fold the arms and legs lengthways right sides together and machine sew the long edge and one short edge of each piece, leaving a 2cm (¾in) seam. Turn all the pieces so the right side is on the outside. A wooden spoon will help you poke the ends of the long pieces through. Do the same for the tail if you are making one.

Sew around the body on the line you have drawn, leaving a gap of about 10cm (4in) on the bottom edge. Turn the right way, fill the body with stuffing and close with stitching. Don't stuff the arms, legs and tail but sew the open ends closed. Hand or machine sew two legs to the bottom of the body, and an arm to either side. Attach the tail to the back.

Using the templates on pages 118–19, cut out a face shape from felt or other material and hand sew on. Add buttons for eyes (if the monkey is for a small child use fabric eyes rather than buttons for safety). Sew a line for a mouth. Sew on the ears.

You can now sew Velcro to the hands if you want your monkey to give you a hug.

Giant bean bags

You will need
- Fleece or fake fur fabric
- Sewing machine
- Polystyrene beads

These can be made from any fleecy fabric or fake fur for extra snugglyness. You can buy big bags of polystyrene beads from our website www.buttonbag.co.uk. It is important not to overfill the bags – they are most comfy when there is extra room inside.

Decide how big you want your beanbag (this will be dictated by the size of your fabric). The ones on the right are between 1 and 2m (39in and 7ft) squares and rectangles. Lay your fabric on the floor and double it over, right sides together. Draw the outline with felt pen. Put some pins through both layers of fabric and cut out at least 2cm (¾in) outside the line you have drawn.

Machine sew around three sides of the rectangle, leaving one of the shorter sides unsewn. Then machine sew over the sewing line at least once more for extra strength. You don't want those polystyrene beads escaping! Turn the bag the right way round.

Ask someone to help you by holding the bag upright, and then tip in the polystyrene beads until the bag is about half to three quarters full, but definitely no fuller than that. Pin across the top and then carefully machine sew closed. Go over over your stitches a couple of times at least.
You can add a tail and some ears for fun, like we did with our tiger stripe bag on pages 36–7.

Mini bean bags

This is a great starter project for the sewing machine but can also be made by hand. Choose different fabrics to add variety.

1. Turn the t-shirt inside out and draw a 12cm (4¾in) square. (It's a good idea to make a paper template first if you want to make more than one.) Cut out.

2. Pin the edges together and machine sew around all four sides 1cm (½in) away from the edge, leaving a 5cm (2in) gap on one edge.

3. Turn the right way out, fill with rice, push the open edges together and top stitch the gap – either on the machine or by hand.

4. Make as many as you want – three is a good number to juggle with.

Jumper monsters

These can be sewn by hand or make an easy starter project for the machine.

- Turn your old jumper inside out and draw a wobbly shape on it with a felt-tip pen. Put some pins through both thicknesses of fabric inside your drawn outline and cut out.
- Sew all round your shape on the sewing machine – use a long stitch setting – about 1cm (½in) away from the edge. Don't worry if the sewing line doesn't follow your cut line exactly – it will add to the character of your monster.
- Turn the right way round and stuff with bits of rag, or cotton wool or soft toy stuffing. Hand-stitch the gap closed.
- Now have fun giving your monster some personality by gluing or sewing on felt eyes, teeth, hair, ears, eyebrows, hands . . . and remember, it's a monster so anything goes!

Fleecy hats

Fleece fabric is easy to cut and sew and has just enough stretch for these simple hats. They can be hand sewn but also make an easy sewing machine project for beginners. The basic pattern can be customized to create loads of different styles. These were inspired by cartoon favourites including Bart Simpson and Batman.

Cut a rectangle of fleece that is as wide as the circumference of your head, plus 2cm (¾in). It should be about 30–40cm (12–16in) high. Fold in half, right sides together, and sew a seam 2cm (¾in) away from the edge.

Turn the right way round and try on. Mark where the top of your head is with a pen. Take off and draw a faint guide line here. Now draw your design for the top – it could be spikes, ears or a fringe. Trim away the excess fabric.

Either sew the top end of the hat closed 2cm (¾in) in from the cut edge – like the bat ears – or simply sew a slight curved line across where you marked the top of your head (Dennis and Bart).

Denim duffel bag

You will need

- Pair of old jeans, the bigger the better.
- Old CD
- Sewing machine
- 2m (7ft) thick cord
- Eyelets (optional)

Denim is a really tough fabric - that's why cowboys loved it. An old pair of adult jeans will give you lots of material to work with. This duffel bag is big enough for all your gear. You can add extra toughness with hammer-in studs (you can buy them from a haberdashery).

1.

Cut both legs off the jeans just above the knee and cut off the bottom hem. Cut off the inside seams to create two big rectangles. Place them right sides together and sew both long edges so you now have one big fat tube.

2.

Turn over about 5cm (2in) at the top and machine sew to make a fabric channel or tunnel. Turn over slightly less at the bottom and machine sew, leaving a gap of about 5cm (2in). Thread the cord through the bottom tunnel (see page 29), pull tight and tie securely.

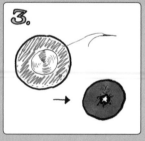

3.

There will be a bit of a hole in the bottom so to stop anything falling out cut a circle of denim about 22cm (9in) in diameter. Hand sew a line of big running stitch about 1cm (½in) from the edge. Place your old CD in the middle and pull the stitches tight so they cover the CD. Tie the threads securely. Place the covered CD inside the bottom of the bag and hold in place with a few big stitches.

4.

Cut the waistband off the jeans and sew it to the top, just below the drawstring tunnel, and the bottom of the bag to make a carrying strap. Cut off one or two of the pockets from the jeans and sew these on to the bag if you like (inside or outside).

5.

Either thread a cord through the top channel (see page 29), or hammer some eyelets through and thread the cord through these.

Toughen up the bag with some hammer-in studs

Easy kit bag

You will need

- Sewing machine
- Old sweatshirt
- 2m (7ft) cord

Turn an old sweatshirt into an easy bag for swimming or PE kit.

1 Turn your sweatshirt inside out and draw a big rectangle. Pin both sides together and cut out.

2 Starting 8cm (3¼in) from the top, machine sew around three sides, 2cm (¾in) from the edge. For extra strength, sew twice on the same line.

3 Snip off the two bottom corners, making sure you don't cut the stitches.

4 Fold down the two top edges, and machine sew them separately to make two channels.

5 Cut two lengths of cord, about 1m (39in) each. See page 29 for how to thread through.

6 Decorate with letters or shapes cut out of felt or fabric. Alternatively, use fabric paints and pens.

Combat lunch bag

Take an old pair of combat style trousers, cut off a piece of the leg big enough to fit your packed lunch in. Better still if it has a pocket on it. Turn it inside out, machine sew around three sides. Turn down a couple of centimetres or inches at the top and machine sew. Turn the right way round. Sew some Velcro on the inside at the top to close it, and some webbing tape on either side to make a strap.

T-shirt bag

Lay an old t-shirt flat on the table. Cut off the sleeves. Cut off the neck. Cut off two 1.5cm (¾in) wide strips from the top of the sleeves and snip the seams so they are one long length. Stretch these two strips. Snip the hem of the t-shirt at the side seams. Attach a safety pin to the end of one of your long pieces and thread this through the front hem (see page 29). Do the same for the back hem. Gather them up and tie tightly.

Gadget cases

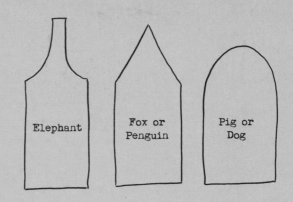

Elephant

Fox or Penguin

Pig or Dog

You will need

- Basic sewing kit
- Fleece fabric or fake fur
- Wiggly eyes, pompoms, buttons for decoration

This **very-easy-to-make** phone or mp3 case can be **customized with an animal face so none of your friends have one the same.**

Cut a rectangular strip of fleece three times as long as your device, and 3cm (1¼in) wider.

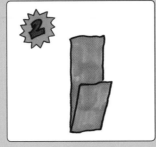

Fold the bottom third of the strip up, measuring against your phone to make sure it will be covered when inside.

Hand sew up either side with an over and over stitch, or a running stitch.

Fold the top flap down and decide what animal to turn it into. Cut the nose/trunk/face shape and add eyes/ears/other features by sewing and sticking. See right for ideas.

Fleece wings
and felt
tummy and
beak

Felt
ears and
pompom
nose

Buttons for snout,
rectangles of fabric
for trotters

Felt
tusks

Button eyes
and wool
whiskers

Play mat bag

You will need

- Fabric – either calico which needs to be machine hemmed or, if you're sewing by hand, a non-frayable material like felt. You need enough for a big circle – about 1m (39in) or up to 1.5m (60in) for a giant circle
- 2m (7ft) strong cotton webbing tape
- Enough cord to go around the circumference with a metre or so to spare
- Basic sewing kit

Imagine all your Lego spread out over the floor so you can find exactly the brick you need - even the little see-through circle things and the laser guns and Indiana Jones' whip. Then with one tug of the cord the whole mat turns into a bag. You can also draw roads on it and use it for cars, and make another one for animals or dinosaurs. You can add rivers or different areas by sewing or drawing on the mat - whatever you like.

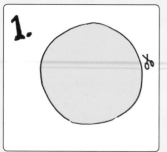

1. Draw a big circle on your fabric and cut out. A pen tied to a piece of string pivoted in the middle of the fabric is the best way to get a big, accurate circle. Hem if necessary.

2. Cut the tape into 12 x 15cm (4¾ x 6in) lengths. Imagine the circle is a clock and mark around the edge at 5, 10, 15, 20 etc. Now fold each piece of tape in half, pin to the circle where marked and hand or machine sew on. Thread the cord through the loops.

3. You can draw roads and buildings on to the fabric or turn your mat into a treasure island. You don't need special pens or paints unless you are planning to wash it – just use felt-tip pens or magic markers.

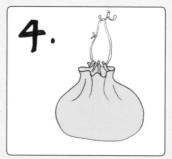

4. Once the bag is gathered up you can hang it on a hook on the door or the wall or just tie the drawstring up and leave on the floor.

PSST !

If you are using a huge dad sock turn it inside out and tie a knot in the toe end to make it shorter, then turn it the right way round. You probably won't need to do this with a smaller sock.

Pinch fabric and sew through cardboard and sock together

Sock puppets

Stripey socks make great sock puppets – black and white for a zebra and technicolour for a dragon.

Cut out ears, eyes and spike shapes using the templates on page 119.

To make the ears stick up, pinch them lengthways down the middle and hand sew a couple of stitches on the fold. Then hand sew them on to the heel of the sock.

To make the dragon spikes stick up, cut out two identical sets of spikes from felt and glue them together, sandwiching the sock inbetween.

Reindeer heads

You will need
- Corrugated cardboard
- Cardboard tube
- Sock
- Buttons, felt or fabric scraps, pipe-cleaners, paper for decorating
- Toy stuffing/cotton wool or fabric scraps

Ever made a sock puppet trophy? You can astound your friends with these amazingly realistic mounted trophies. Rudolphs look great for Christmas but stripey socks make great zebras and you could do lions, warthogs – just see what's lurking in your sock drawer.

Cut a cardboard shield shape – stick two together to make it more three-dimensional. This one is 30cm (12in) high and about 28cm (11in) wide.

Cut a diagonal slice off the cardboard tube. Place the cut end on the middle of the shield and draw around it.

Cut out the circle in the shield. Now cut slots all around the cut end of the tube.

Sew or stick a button or a circle of red fabric or paper to the toe end of the sock. Stuff the sock with stuffing, cotton wool or rags to just about where the ankle would go.

Sew or stick on eyes, ears and antlers. If you don't have any pipe cleaners cut out antler shapes from cardboard or find a couple of suitable twigs in the park.

Now push the cardboard tube in to form the neck. Push through the hole in the shield. Fan out the slots to help it stay in place and tuck any excess sock back into the cardboard tube. It should be snug enough to stay in place – if not, use some strong sticky tape or glue to hold in place.

CREEPY CRAFT

Rats
p.59

Creepy craft

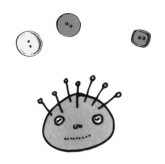

Making creepy costumes and scary accessories is the best bit of Halloween. But don't save these projects for one night only – creepy craft is good at any time of the year. The bouncy spiders and rats are easy hand-sewing projects and the weapons and eyeballs don't take long to make. Dead man's finger is a classic kid's trick and was popular long before trick or treating became the norm. See how realistic you can make it.

Zombies

Zombies are about the easiest Halloween costume. You can put a pretty scary outfit together in a few minutes and you can also zombify existing costumes - like a zombie pirate or zombie cowboy.

Take an old t-shirt, shirt or jumper, cut some holes with a pair of scissors and splatter with fake blood or red paint. You can do the same with a pair of trousers, but it's not essential.

Make an impressive fake axe from sturdy cardboard and an old broom handle or a thick stick. Spray the blade with silver or gold paint, or wrap it in tin foil. Tie it to the handle with string or an elastic band. Smear fake blood, red paint or even red nail varnish on the edge for a gruesome bloody finish.

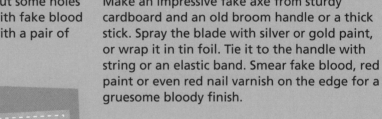

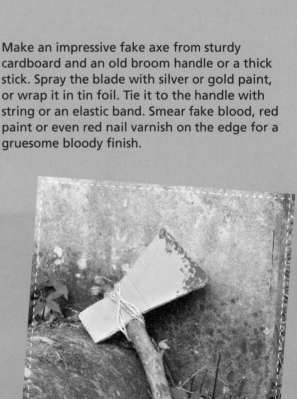

Spiders

You will need

- Fabric
- Toy stuffing
- Pipe cleaners
- Wiggly eyes
- Basic sewing kit

Make these spiders even more creepy by sewing on scary faces with embroidery thread. You can make them from any scraps of fabric - fleece, felt - or cut up an old jumper or t-shirt.

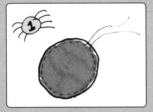

Use a plate to draw a circle on your fabric and cut out. Using thick thread sew some longish stitches all around the circle, about 1cm (½in) from the edge.

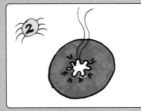

Pull the threads tight to gather up the fabric, push some stuffing in through the gap and then tie the threads in a knot.

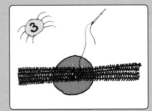

Take 4 pipe cleaners and lie them across the gathered bit of the spider's body. Using big stitches sew them across the middle.

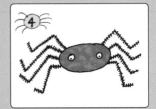

Shape the pipe cleaners into legs and add some eyes, eyebrows, teeth and any other details. You can also sew some elastic on to the top of your spider.

Rats

You will need

- Soft fabric – about a 20cm (8in) square
- Basic sewing kit
- Toy stuffing
- Pipe cleaners
- Wiggly eyes (optional)

If you don't have any fleece fabric you could cut up an old jumper or t-shirt to make these rats. You could also use string or wool for the tails instead of pipe cleaners.

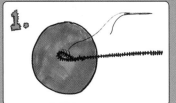

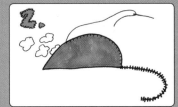

Use a plate to draw a circle on your fabric and cut out.
Make a small loop at one end of the pipe-cleaner and secure to the middle of the circle with a couple of stitches.

Fold the circle in half and sew around the edge using an over and over stitch. Stop about 5cm (2in) before the end and push stuffing through the gap. Finish sewing, closing the gap.

Cut two fabric triangles for ears and sew on. Embroider eyes or stick on wiggly eyes or other eye shapes cut from felt or paper.

Bats

You will need

- Black paper
- Old-fashioned wooden clothes pegs (craft shops often have these)
- White chalk or pencil
- Black felt pen or paint
- Elastic or string

This is a really simple way to make spooky bats. Tie them on to a piece of elastic and hang in the window or a doorframe to fly.

Copy or trace the batwing template on page 120 on to black paper and cut out. Draw bone detail with white chalk or a pencil.

Thread the wings on to the clothes peg.

Draw on a bat face and colour in the body of the peg with black. Tie elastic or string around the top half of the body leaving enough spare to hang your bat (or you can always tie on an extra piece).

Dead man's finger

You will need

- An empty match box
- Flour and water, or white paint
- Tissue
- Red paint, felt tip pen or tomato ketchup

This is a classic trick. When you are showing people your dead man's finger think up a good cover story and tell it with a straight face.

1.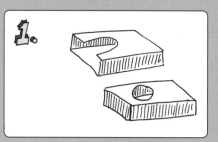

Cut a hole in the tray of the match box large enough to fit your finger. Cut a slot in the sleeve. Put it back together and have a go at putting your finger in, closing and opening the lid.

2.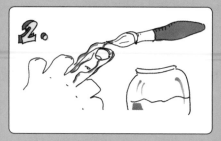

Mix a tablespoon of flour and water together into a thick paste and paint on to your finger. As it dries it will go flaky and help give the illusion of dead skin.

3.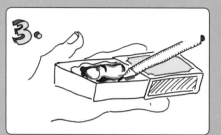

Put a little tissue in the box making sure you don't obstruct the hole and paint liberally with red pen, paint or tomato ketchup. Now poke your finger through and close the box.
Think up a spooky story – practise a couple of times and then 'reveal' your finger to your audience.

Egg eyeballs

Hardboil and peel some eggs – small ones are best. Draw on a spooky eyeball with a felt tip pen. Produce your egg eyeball from your pocket along with a terrifying tale about how you found it – think full moons, werewolves, school dinners. Pop it in an empty jam jar or a large matchbox to keep it safe.

Vampire cloak

You will need

- Rectangle of fabric 1m (39in) wide by however long you want the cloak. If you use a fraying fabric you will need to hem the sides and the bottom.
- ½m (2in) thick elastic, about 3cm (1¼in) wide
- 6cm (2¼in) sew-on Velcro
- 2 safety pins
- Basic sewing kit
- Sewing machine
- Ribbon (optional)

The high ruffed neck makes this a great vampire cloak - but it also works well for wizards, witches and any other dressing up larks. The long straight lines of sewing mean it really is best to do this one on a sewing machine, however you can try hand sewing if you prefer.

Fold and pin a 12cm (4¾) wide hem along one side of the fabric.

Machine sew two parallel lines along the hem at least 1cm (½in) wider than the elastic. If you are hand sewing, keep your stitches very straight.

Using a large safety pin, thread the elastic through the channel and gather up the fabric until it just fits around your neck with about 8cm (3¼in) of elastic sticking out on each side. Use safety pins to hold the elastic in place while you sew it securely down with two vertical lines of sewing. Remove the pins.

Sew the Velcro to the two ends of the elastic.

You can tie the ribbon in a bow and sew on to the other side of the elastic (optional).

Turn an old red t-shirt into a sleek red waistcoat any vampire would be proud to flash beneath its cloak. Cut off the arms and neck and draw a line up the front and black buttons with a magic marker.

Evil heads

Turn the paper sculpture heads (see page 12) into part of your Halloween costume with a bit of elastic or just put them in the window for a creepy decoration. Paint the scariest most horrific face possible – crazed zombie/vampire/devil is a good option as it can incorporate any papery lumps and bumps.

Make an evil twin by putting the head on your shoulder and securing it with an elastic band around your armpit. Cut a hole just big enough for the base in the shoulder seam of your top and poke the head through.

Make two holes in the base of the yoghurt pot neck with a sharp pair of scissors. Thread a bit of thick elastic through and measure enough so it is a snug fit around your chin.

Disguise the neck and your face with a cloak, a big shirt, a coat or a sheet. Either leave a gap to see through or – if you're using a sheet – just cut some holes for your eyes.

Master of disguise

Create an instant disguise or alter ego! Using the template on pages 120–21, cut out a beard or moustache shape from fake fur or fleece fabric. It's much easier if you draw the shape on the non-furry side first. Attach it with double-sided sticky tape.

Eyebrows come in all shapes and sizes – cut according to your inspiration. You can always attach some hairy eyebrows to an old pair of glasses.

WARNING!

Try and avoid sticking to your own hair or eyebrows and be very careful when you remove the tape. Firstly because it hurts, and secondly because you might end up with some embarrassing bald patches.

WOOD CRAFT

Little log
bugs p.78

Working with wood

Sawing planks of wood can be hard work. But wood craft doesn't need to be about perfect carpentry. These stick creatures below take you straight to the fun bit – banging nails into bits of wood. If you want to make something a bit more sturdy, like the log bug or the bird box, you may want to get some help with the sawing.

Stick craft

Glue, tie or nail sticks together to create lots of imaginary animals, insects, tiny rafts, chairs, wigwams and other structures. Use a hacksaw or sturdy secaturs to saw or chop the sticks into different lengths. You don't need to go anywhere special – your local park or even the trees on your street should shed plenty of suitable twiggy offerings.

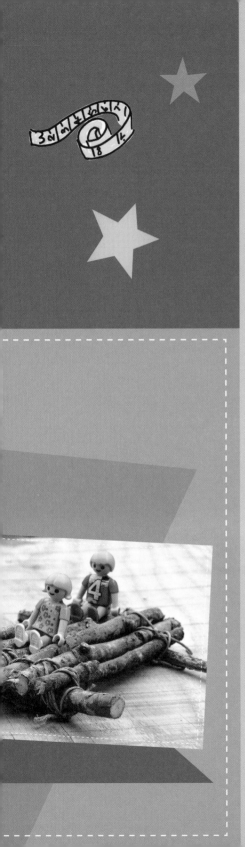

Stilts

Ask a grown up to help you with this. You will need two lengths of wood about as tall as you are, and two blocks of wood which are big enough to put your feet on. The wood needs to be sturdy enough to hold you. Hammer the two blocks on to the long bits of wood about 30cm (12in) from the bottom, or higher if you are feeling brave. Make sure they are securely attached before climbing on.

Bug hotel

You will need

- Bamboo canes
- Small piece of wood
- Glue
- String

These have become very popular and you can buy fancy versions at garden centres. You can make a really simple one with some bamboo and a small offcut of wood.

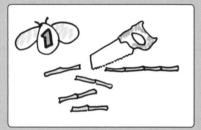

Saw the bamboo into short lengths all roughly around 10cm (4in) long.

Using wood glue, stick the first row of bamboo lengths on to a wooden base. Carefully glue another row on top. You may have to wait until the glue is dry if the bamboo starts to slip.

Build up rows in the same way so you end up with a pyramid. Slip a loop of string round the last piece of bamboo before sticking into place if you want to hang it from a tree or fence.

Bird box

You will need
- Plank of wood
- 12 screws
- Small hinge
- Small length of dowel (optional)

This bird box is made from a single plank of pine flooring and is easy to construct once you have all the pieces cut. You will probably need to get an adult to help you saw the wood up.

1. Look at the template below and, adjusting the size to fit your plank, mark all the pieces on to the plank. Remember that the floor and the roof are the width of the plank plus twice the thickness. Our plank was 11cm (4¼in) wide, so our floor and roof was 11 + (2 x 1.5)cm = 14cm (5½in).

2. Saw the pieces and label each one with a pencil so you know which is which. With an adult helping you drill two holes on each side of the sides and one on each side of the bottom. Drill an extra hole near the top of the long back piece so you can hang the bird box on a nail, and one on the front edge of the roof. Drill a hole with a 3cm (1¼in) diameter in one of the side pieces so the birds can go in and out. If you are making a perch drill a hole the same width as your dowel, or simply hammer in a long nail for a perch.

3. Sand off any rough cut edges. Screw the bottom, back and sides together using a wood bench to help you hold the pieces still – you may want to work out where the screws go into the edge of the front and side pieces and drill small guide holes.

4. Place the roof on the box and mark where the holes for the hinge go. Screw it in place. You can varnish, paint or leave plain.

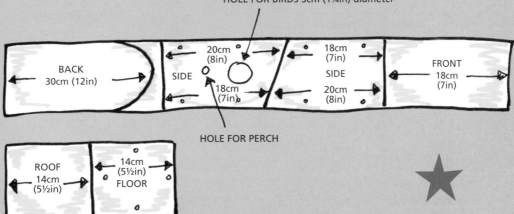

HOLE FOR BIRDS 3cm (1¼in) diameter

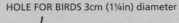

BACK 30cm (12in)

SIDE

20cm (8in)

18cm (7in)

SIDE

18cm (7in)

20cm (8in)

FRONT 18cm (7in)

HOLE FOR PERCH

ROOF 14cm (5½in)

14cm (5½in) FLOOR

Little log bugs

With thanks to Hampshire grandad Richard for this project. This pull-along creature is made from little logs and/or sticks found in the wood pile or forest. Make sure your wood isn't rotten though. And while this woodwork project is simple, most children will need an adult to help them with the sawing and the drilling.

Saw logs and sticks to make the body, axles and wheels. At one end of the body saw a diagonal piece off to make the face.

Drill a hole in the centre of each wheel, and a hole in the middle of each axle to attach it to the body.

Screw a wheel on to the end of each axle. Leave the screws quite loose so the wheels will turn round.

Screw the axles to the underneath of the body about 5cm (2in) from either end.

Draw or mark a face on the diagonally sliced end of the body. Attach the string for pulling with a U-shaped nail.

MODEL CRAFT

Action heroes
p.90

Chariot
p.88

Model making

Most of the models to make in this book started life in the recycling bin. Don't think of it as rubbish but as a huge source of brilliant craft materials. Milk bottle plastic is particularly good for craft. It's soft and easy to cut with regular scissors and you can paint it with any kind of paint. Jam Jar lids are a great base for medals – or miniature wheels or shields. Cereal boxes will provide all the thin cardboard you need and your local shop or supermarket will usually give you a corrugated cardboard box if you can't find one at home.

PAINTS
Household emulsion is good to use as a base coat. Little pots of enamel paint are great for details and so are the Citadel model paints you can buy in model shops. Spray paint can give your projects a really professional look. Although they are expensive you don't need a huge range of colours to make a big difference. Gold, silver and red are good ones to start with.

GLUE
PVA glue is good enough for most paper and card. It's worth using copydex (be warned – it smells of dead fish) for fabrics or another specialised textile glue. For stronger glues we use plastic model-making glue – the kind you get with a model aircraft kit, or for making Warhammer figures. Never be tempted to use superglue – the only thing you're likely to stick together is your fingers.

CUTTING
Most of these projects don't require any tools sharper than a pair of scissors. Really tough cardboard – like the inner tube from a foil roll – can be sawed (like a log) using a bread knife and a chopping board. Sometimes the top of a plastic bottle can be really tough. Ask an adult to saw it off with a small hacksaw (or a bread knife if they can't find one).

Jam jar medals

These medals can be made for sporting winners or to commemorate something historically important like the moon landing, a coronation, or your next birthday, or make them as a gift for someone special. Draw around a jam jar lid on some paper a few times and sketch out some ideas for your medal design. You can make up your design or copy something you've seen.

If the lid has printing on it give it a coat of paint so you have a blank canvas and let it dry. Spray paint is a good option here. Draw or paint your design. If it's very complicated, a thin permanent marker pen can help you get a more accurate outline. When it's completely dry, firmly tape a piece of ribbon to the other side to form a loop that can go around your neck.

Egyptian mummies

Cut a small plastic drinking bottle in half vertically. Trim the top down if necessary to give a better sarcophagus shape.

Cover both halves with papier mache (see page 11) and add a thin layer to the inside too. You may want to pad the 'shoulders' with extra papier mache.

Paint the entire outer surface and when dry use a pen to mark out your basic design. Copy the design below or make up your own.

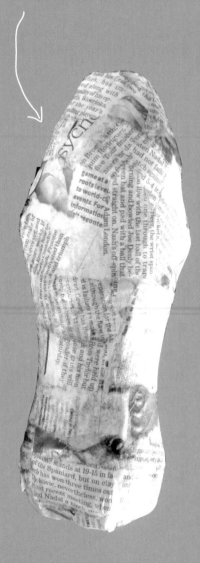

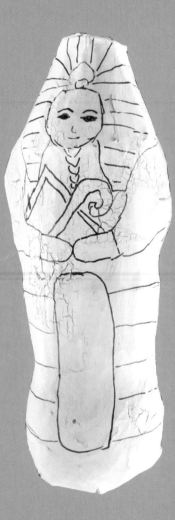

You can use any kind of paint – we used a mixture of household emulsion for the base, enamel model paint, Citadel paints (from Warhammer), gold spray paint and then added fine detail with a gold pen.

Make a mummy by taping a pencil to a mummy shape cut out of cardboard. Then wrap the whole thing in a thin strip of white material. You could cut strips from an old sheet or t-shirt or just use toilet paper.

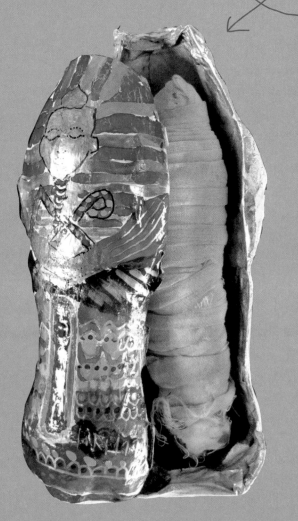

Pyramid money box

You will need

- Thick corrugated cardboard
- Sticky tape
- Paint
- Glue
- Sharp scissors or craft knife
- Plastic lid from cocoa carton, thin cardboard, sand (optional)

1

15cm
22cm

(15cm=6in
22cm=8½in)

Draw the shape shown above on to corrugated cardboard. Cut out and gently score the sides of the square (the base of the pyramid). Cut a coin-sized slot half-way up one side.

2

Push the triangular sides up to form a pyramid and tape together.

If you like to take your pocket money out and count it regularly, or you spend it almost as soon as you get it, you will definitely want to put a lid in the bottom of this money box. But you can make it without a lid and wait until you've saved up a huge hoard before finally cutting the pyramid open to reveal the treasure buried within.

3

You can cut some thin cardboard (a cereal packet is ideal) into strips about 2cm (¾in) wide. Cut the strips into rectangles. Stick these on to the pyramid to make it look like it's been built from solid blocks. (Optional)

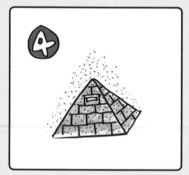

4

If you want to decorate it, you can paint the pyramid or brush with glue all over and sprinkle with fine dry sand.

TRY THIS!
If you want to be able to take
money out and count it without
destroying your pyramid, in step 1,
carefully draw around the cocoa lid
in the middle of the square base.
Cut out using a sharp pair of
scissors or a craft knife.
The cocoa lid should fit
very snugly.

Chariot

Plastic milk bottles can be cut down to make all kinds of vehicles. They make particularly impressive old world chariots. Decorate with hieroglyphics for an Egyptian look or if you are feeling ambitious add battle scenes for a Roman look.

Draw a chariot shape on to the bottom end of a clean empty plastic bottle. You can research different chariot shapes on the internet – search 'roman chariot', for example. Cut out and paint. Spray paints work well for a fast-drying smooth finish. When dry add details and decoration with permanent marker pens.

Make wheels from cardboard or use jam jar lids. Use a wooden skewer for an axle and either push it through holes in the bottom of the chariot shape, or thread through a straw taped firmly to the underside of the chariot.

Make stays for the horse by pushing very thin twigs through two holes in the front of the chariot and securing to a plastic animal with an elastic band.

Action heroes

Turn old action figures into characters from history. You will just need a few scraps of fabric for the clothes and you can create all kinds of weapons, hats and other bits of gear for them from the recycling box. For example, the Viking's shield is a jam jar lid and Pharaoh King's headpiece is the top of a washing-up liquid bottle. Look at the basic patterns in the template section on pages 122-5.

You don't need to sew sleeveless tunics; simply cut a hole for the head and tie around the body with wool or string. If you prefer to sew, these are all better sewn by hand rather than machine. The trouser pattern can be adjusted to make trousers of any size - even for you.

Pharaoh King

KILT: Short piece of white fabric wrapped and tied at the waist with ribbon.

HEADDRESS: Cut the top off a washing-up liquid bottle with a sharp pair of scissors. Ask an adult to saw the very top bit off. Cut two vertical lines upwards, one each side of the width of the face. Fold this piece back and trim to about a third. Spray gold and decorate with paint.

NECKPIECE: Using the template on page 122, cut out of a plastic milk bottle, spray gold and decorate.

WRIST GUARDS: Wrap a strip of black paper around the wrist and decorate with sequins (glue or fix with a couple of stitches).

SANDALS: Draw these on with gold pen.

Egyptian Princess

ROBE: Cut a sleeveless tunic out of white fabric using the template on page 122. Tie with string or ribbon.

HEADDRESS: Cut out of gold card or plastic milkbottle and spray gold.

NECKPIECE: Using the template on page 122, cut out of a plastic milk bottle and spray gold.

SANDALS AND BRACELETS: Draw these on with a gold pen.

Roman centurion

SLEEVELESS TUNIC: Cut one from brown fabric and one from white (see template on page 122). From the waist down cut vertical strips in the brown tunic to create flaps. Put the brown tunic over the white one. Roman tunics were generally above the knee.

CLOAK: Cut from red felt (see template on page 124). Epaulettes are cut from pieces of gold card.

SHIELD: Cut the handle off a small plastic milk bottle. Cut a shield shape from another piece of the milk bottle. We chose a section with horizontal indents to add some detail. Spray silver and staple or glue the shield and handle together.

HELMET: Cut the lid off a small oval plastic bottle – this one was nail varnish remover but baby bubble bath is another good option. Spray silver. Cut two plume shapes from red felt or card and sandwich together. Glue these together leaving about 5mm from the edge so they can be splayed and glued over the top of the bottle. Make evenly spaced cuts vertically from the top to create a 'feathered' look.

SANDALS: Draw these on with a marker pen.

Viking warrior

BEARD AND HAIR: Glue on small pieces of fake fur fabric.

SLEEVELESS TUNIC: Use fake fur and cut out using the template on page 122. Tie on with string.

TROUSERS: Use template on page 125 and tie around the bottom with wool.

HELMET: This is the top of a plastic bottle covered with foil. The horns are made from modelling clay and glued on.

SHIELD: This is a painted jam jar lid with a pipe cleaner handle taped to the inside.

SWORD: Use the template on page 124 and cut out of silver card or a plastic milk bottle sprayed silver.

Henry VIII

BEARD AND EYEBROWS: Glue on small pieces of fake fur.

BODY: Wind a strip of fleece fabric around the body a few times to bulk him up (or you can go without and have a young Henry).

CLOAK: Cut velvet fabric using the template on page 124. Decorate with white fabric or fleece and use a black marker to create ermine-link spots.

SLEEVELESS TUNIC: Cut velvet fabric using the template on page 122. Decorate with glued on glitzy trim and jewel-like sequins.

LEGGINGS: Tubular finger bandages are cut to size (tie on with string if needed).

SHOES: Use the template on page 122 to make these with black felt and gold card buckles.

HAT: Cut two ovals of black fleece using the template on page 122 and decorate with diamante studs attached with glue.

SHOULDER FRILLS: Take a metal scouring ball and pull apart to reveal hole in middle and put over each arm.

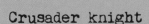

Crusader knight

TUNIC WITH SLEEVES: Use the template on page 123 to make up the tunic.

TROUSERS: Use the template on page 125 to make these. You can use the same fabric as the tunic or choose something different.

TABARD: Use white cloth and cut using the sleeveless tunic template on page 122. Stick gold ribbon around the edges and draw the crusader's cross design with red pen. Fasten with red wool or cord.

CHAINMAIL: Use a metallic fabric or netting from bags of fruit (spray with metallic paint or use it as it comes) to make a chainmail tunic (see the template on page 123). Wrap a rectangular piece of metallic fabric or netting around his head (glue or add a stitch to hold in place).

CROWN: Cut a small piece of gold card and glue to fit.

Elastic band car

You will need

- Sturdy cardboard tube, such as a from a roll of foil
- Drinking straw
- Wooden skewers
- Plastic lids for wheels
- Glue
- Thick elastic band
- Plastic milk bottle to cut up for the nose and tail

Elastic bands have been silently powering thousands of junk box cars across pavements and living rooms for decades. Once you've mastered the technology you can adapt it to your own vehicle design. Think of this one as a starting point. You'll find lots of other ideas on the internet on maker's forums.

Although simple in design, it can be quite tricky to get these cars to run properly because if the axles aren't straight, or the wheels aren't fixed really securely to the axles, they won't turn.

Make two holes at opposite ends of the cardboard tube and insert two short lengths of drinking straw.

Push short lengths of a wooden skewer through the straws and attach wheels to each end. Plastic milk bottle and jar lids (peanut butter!) are good here. Put them on a wooden board and pierce the centre with a sharp skewer, knitting needle or nail. Then push on to the skewer. They should stay, but if not, glue with a blob of strong plastic model making glue.

Push a third short skewer through the tube about three quarters of the way down. This should be really snug – you may want to glue it in place. Cut a thick elastic band into a long strip and tie one end to this skewer and one end to the back axle. You can experiment with a second elastic band on the other side too.

To run your car, turn the back axle to wind the elastic tight, then put it on the ground and release.

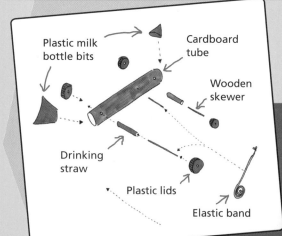

Plastic milk bottle bits

Cardboard tube

Wooden skewer

Drinking straw

Plastic lids

Elastic band

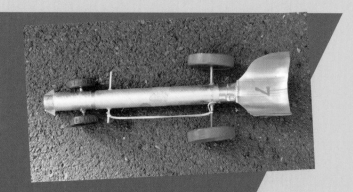

Balloon car

You will need

- Large match box or a small square of cardboard for the base
- 2 drinking straws
- Milk carton lids
- Wooden skewer
- Balloon

Use wind power to propel a junk box car across the floor. The body of the car can be made from any kind of box – the trick is to angle the bendy straw upwards to keep the balloon off the floor. Remember, the car will go in the direction of the balloon.

Tape two pieces of straw to the base of the matchbox.
  Cut two axles from wooden skewers a little wider than the box, push through the straw and fix a wheel on each end (as for the Elastic band car opposite).
  Cut the lip off the balloon and tape the balloon firmly to the bendy end of the straw. Bend the straw upwards and tape to the top of the box. Trim the other end of the straw leaving enough so you can blow through it to inflate the balloon. Decorate it if you like.
  Blow up the balloon, set the car on the ground and watch it go!

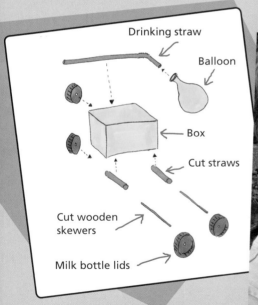

Drinking straw

Balloon

Box

Cut straws

Cut wooden skewers

Milk bottle lids

WACKY RACES

Hold your own Wacky Rally with your friends and race your fastest cars against each other. Use jam jar lids, milk bottle tops, cotton reels, buttons, old CDs or discs cut from card for the wheels and anything you like for the body. The Batmobile was made by taping straw axles to the bottom of a plastic drink bottle. Design a sign and a chequered flag and get set to go!

PSST!
The axle has to
turn freely for
the wheels to
go round.

Peg doll figures

You will need
- Old-fashioned wooden clothes pegs – available from craft suppliers and our website www.buttonbag.co.uk
- Pipe cleaners
- Sticky tape
- Scraps of fabric, wool, etc.

Just like your grandma used to make – only much more fun. Peg knights, wizards, pirates, Robin Hood . . . be inspired by your Lego or Playmobil characters.

Push a pipe cleaner through peg legs. Twist diagonally to each side of the body to make arms. Secure with a piece of sticky tape wrapped securely round the body. Fold each end of the pipe cleaner back on itself and twist firmly to make a sort of hand shape.

See the templates on page 126 for ideas for characters to make. Most things can be wrapped and tied around the peg. If you want to be fancy, try sewing very small seams with very small stitches.

Stick on wool for hair, draw on faces with coloured pencils or pen. Make crowns, swords and shields from gold card.

Super hero softies

Turn your favourite stuffed animals into a crack team of crime-fighting heroes.

Make eye masks and capes from small fabric scraps. Design a logo or symbol for each one, cut out of card and hang it around their neck on a ribbon or a string, or draw the logo on to a cape.

Santa sleigh

This is a **Christmassy** version of the ancient
Egyptian chariots on page 88 and looks great on
your Christmas table, window sill or mantelpiece.

Cut down a 2 litre plastic milk bottle to give a sledge shape.
Spray it red and decorate with gold pen. Cut runners from card,
paint them silver and stick them to the side of the sledge.

Father Christmas is a small teddy bear with some cotton wool
stuck on for a beard. To make a Father Christmas hat draw a
segment of a circle – about a third – on some red fabric or paper.
Use the base of a large mug or small plate to help you. Cut out,
shape into a cone and tape or sew the straight edges together.

The reindeer is a toy donkey with a small piece of red
lego stuck on his nose and some antlers made from a black
pipe-cleaner.

Fill the sledge with sweets and chocolates.

Glitter jar

Use an empty jam jar to make an old-fashioned snow globe.

Make a tiny scene out of modelling clay – perhaps Santa at the South Pole or some trees covered in snow. Glue it into the inside of the lid of your jar, which will be the base for your snow globe. Leave until the glue is completely dry. Fill the jar with water and add a tablespoon of glitter. You can add a drop of food colouring too if you like. Make sure the lid is tightly back on the jar and shake!

Underwater scenes are perfect for these jars too

Christmas wreath

There's no sewing involved in this Christmas wreath.

Bend a wire coat hanger into a vaguely round shape. Cut some fabric strips about 5 x 12cm (2 x 4¾in) in size from old t-shirts, tracksuit bottoms, school jumpers, scarfs or left-over materials. No need to measure them exactly – just do it by eye. Tie each one round the coathangar until it is completely covered. Trim or fluff up the ends if necessary. You can leave it plain or decorate with sweets, Christmas decorations or pine cones. Wrapped up sweets can be tied on with short lengths of string or thread.

Teddy angels

Christmas decorations don't have to be boring.

Cut some angel wings out of thick corrugated cardboard (see template on page 127), spray them gold or silver and decorate with glitter and sequins. Use elastic bands to attach them to the teddies and thread a piece of tinsel through the back to hang them up. They also make great fairies for the top of the tree.

WOOLLY CRAFT

Finger knitting
p.110

How to: Knit

Think knitting's just for grannies? Think again! Try finger knitting a cool scarf. No needles needed – just use your fingers. Be warned though, it's addictive.

   Once you've mastered the finger stuff, have a go at the real thing. Think of knitting as a series of knots – a chain of knots that are all linked together – a bit like chainmail. And while you won't find a recipe here for a chainmail suit, you don't have to stick to wool. You can cut up plastic bags and knit with them or even a t-shirt for a really chunky scarf.

Casting on
There are lots of different ways to cast on and it's great if a friend or a relative shows you their favourite method. This is the Buttonbag method – also known as 'cable edge'.

RH = right hand LH = left hand

STEP ONE
Tie a double knot loosely around one needle. Hold this in your left hand. Hold the yarn from the ball and the second needle in your right hand. Push the pointed end of RH needle through the loop under the LH needle.

STEP TWO
Wrap the yarn around point of the RH needle and hold fairly snug (wind it once around your RH index finger).

STEP THREE
Holding the yarn firm, slide the RH needle back towards you under the LH needle and through the original stitch. The yarn you just wound around the RH needle is now a new stitch on the RH needle.

STEP FOUR
Push the tip of the LH needle through the new stitch on the RH needle and slide it off and on to the LH needle.

STEP FIVE
To make the third, and all following stitches push needle between first and second stitches and repeat steps 2 to 4. All knitting patterns will tell you how many stitches to cast on.

Knit stitch

When you work every row using this stitch it is called 'garter stitch'. It is the simplest kind of knitted fabric you can make.

STEP ONE
Hold the needle with the stitches in your left hand. Push the point of the RH needle up into the first stitch from the front to the back. Let go of the RH needle and wrap the yarn around the back of the RH needle and then between the tips of the two needles. Holding the yarn firm in your RH, wrap it round your index finger again, slide the RH needle back towards you under the LH needle and through the original stitch so the wound-round yarn is now a new stitch on the RH needle.

STEP TWO
Slide the RH needle up the LH needle until the old stitch slips off the tip. You've now knitted your first stitch.

STEP THREE
Repeat for every stitch on the LH needle. You've now knitted your first row. Swap the needles over so the one with the stitches is now in your LH. Keep on doing this until your knitting is long enough. All knitting patterns will either tell you how many rows or centimetres you need.

Casting off

When you've finished knitting you need to get all the stitches off the needle in a way that ensures they don't unravel. This is 'casting off'.

STEP ONE
Knit two stitches. Push the tip of the LH needle through the first stitch you knitted on the RH needle and pull it back over the top of the second stitch and off the needle. You will have just one stitch left on your RH needle. Knit another stitch so that you have two stitches again and repeat as above until the end of the row.

STEP TWO
When you have one stitch left on the RH needle, cut the yarn leaving a tail of about 20cm (8in). Using your finger, loosen the final stitch so it becomes a big loop and push the end of the yarn though and pull tight.

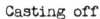

Finger knitting

You will need
• Wool – that's all!

The ultimate portable craft. This is a great way to make cool scarves, bracelets and headbands. No equipment is needed except your fingers and some wool. By using more than one strand of wool at a time you can make a thick multi-coloured rope. You can also knit your strands together to make your scarf even chunkier.

1. Tie anywhere between one and four pieces of yarn around your left-hand thumb and, holding your hand up with your palm towards you, weave it loosely in front of your first finger, behind the next, in front of the next, round your little finger and back to thumb. Now take the yarn across all your fingers so it lies just above the first layer of loops. Leave the thumb alone. It just acts as the anchor.

2. Using your right hand, grab the first loop of wool on your first finger and take it over the wool that's lying just above it and right over your finger. Do the same with the wool loops on the other three fingers.

3. Take the yarn all the way round the back of your fingers and over the front again. Repeat steps 2 and 3 about ten times.

4. Now take the wool off your thumb and pull gently down at the back. You can see the knitted tube beginning to form. Just keep repeating steps two and three until it is as long as you want.

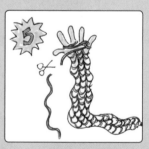

5. Cut off the yarn leaving a tail about 20cm (8in) long. Thread the tail through each stitch in turn, starting with the little finger and slipping them off as you go.

Eco knitting

This is a good way to recycle plastic bags into something that you can keep.

We made ours into cuffs, but you could always turn them into drink or table mats too. Cut any handles off your plastic bag. Then, starting at the top, cut one continuous spiral and then wind into a ball. For the cuff, cast on 10 stitches and knit enough rows to make a strip long enough to go over your hand and around your wrist, about 20cm (8in). Cast off and sew together using a needle with a big eye.

T-shirt scarf

We cut up some old t-shirts and turned them into a chunky warm scarf. Try knitting on the biggest needles you can find to make it quicker and easier. Cut a t-shirt into a long strip, about 1.5cm (½in) wide (you don't have to be too accurate) by starting at the hem and spiralling all the way up to the top. Wind this strip into a ball so it doesn't get all tangled up. To make our scarf we cast on 15 stitches, and knitted 6 t-shirts on big needles. When you are nearly at the end of one t-shirt, knot the end to the next t-shirt strip and carry on. Cast off when your scarf is long enough. You could also knit three strips and then sew them together to make a rug.

Knitted pets

If a scarf is going to take too long to make,
try a knitted pet instead . . .

These knitted creatures are made by folding a very small knitted
rectangle in half. Sew up the sides, stuff, sew the top closed and
decorate with felt scraps, pompoms, sticky eyes, buttons (unless it's
for a baby or toddler) or whatever else you feel like using.

Pink

10 stitches, 40 rows

Yellow

15 stitches, 50 rows

PURPLE

12 stitches, 20 rows

Green

15 stitches, 24 rows

Blue

12 stitches, 24 rows

Templates

You can photocopy these templates to use for your craft projects.

p.20 Medals for bravery

The George Cross

1939–1945 Star

Victoria Cross

British war medal
1914–1920

p.30 Jumper monkeys

Make the faces
about twice this
size, depending
on how big
your monkey
turns out.

Cut faces out of felt, use buttons
for eyes (unless it's for a baby or
toddler) and embroider or draw
mouth detail.

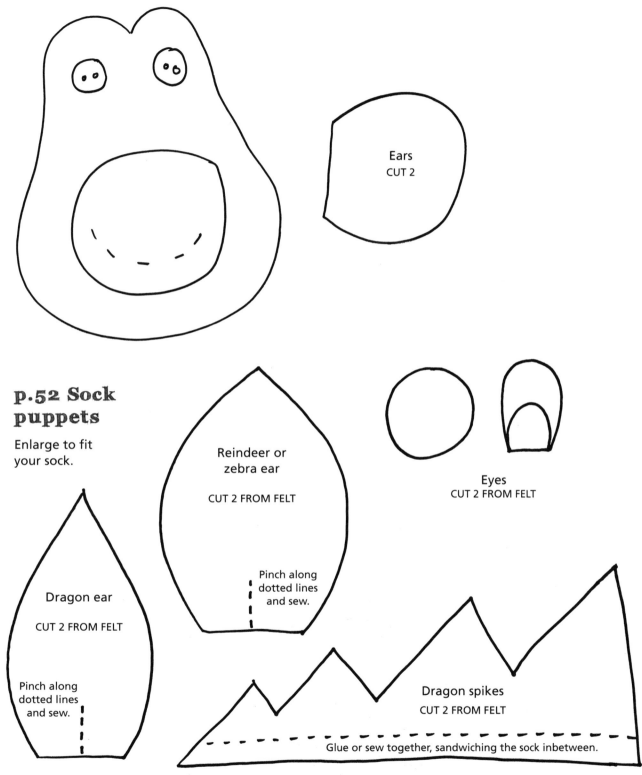

p.52 Sock puppets

Enlarge to fit
your sock.

Ears
CUT 2

Reindeer or
zebra ear

CUT 2 FROM FELT

Eyes
CUT 2 FROM FELT

Pinch along
dotted lines
and sew.

Dragon ear

CUT 2 FROM FELT

Pinch along
dotted lines
and sew.

Dragon spikes

CUT 2 FROM FELT

Glue or sew together, sandwiching the sock inbetween.

Make as long as your sock puppet neck.

p.60 Bats   Make the wings about twice this size.

p.68 Master of disguise

Here are some ideas for fake beards, moustaches and eyebrows for you to copy. You'll need to enlarge them to the right size to fit your face.

pp.90–93 Action heroes

Lots of patterns are cut on a folded piece of fabric. This can help get both sides of your shape exactly the same. So it's always important to see if there are any markings on the pattern saying 'fold'. Try to keep your stitches neat and the same length – about 5mm.

Pharaoh King and Egyptian Princess neckpieces

Place the pattern on the side of a milk bottle so that the hole for the neck and shoulders is on the edge. This makes it fit around the figure's shoulders really well.

Henry's shoes
CUT 2 FROM FELT AND STITCH

Henry VIII's hat

CUT 2 FROM FLEECE OR FELT

FOLD   FOLD

Sleeveless tunic

Cut out and tie on.
Don't worry about hemming.

Egyptian Princess
Roman centurion
Viking warrior
Henry VIII
Crusader knight

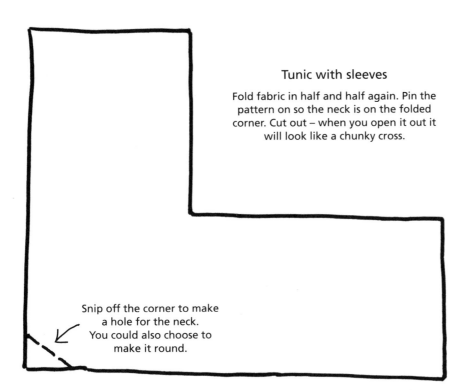

Tunic with sleeves

Fold fabric in half and half again. Pin the pattern on so the neck is on the folded corner. Cut out – when you open it out it will look like a chunky cross.

Snip off the corner to make a hole for the neck. You could also choose to make it round.

SEWING UP THE TUNIC

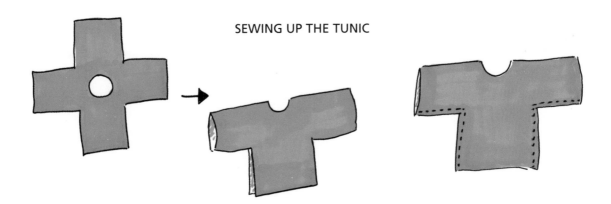

Fold the cross in half and then sew up the bottom of the sleeves and down the sides. Remember to leave the holes for the arms!

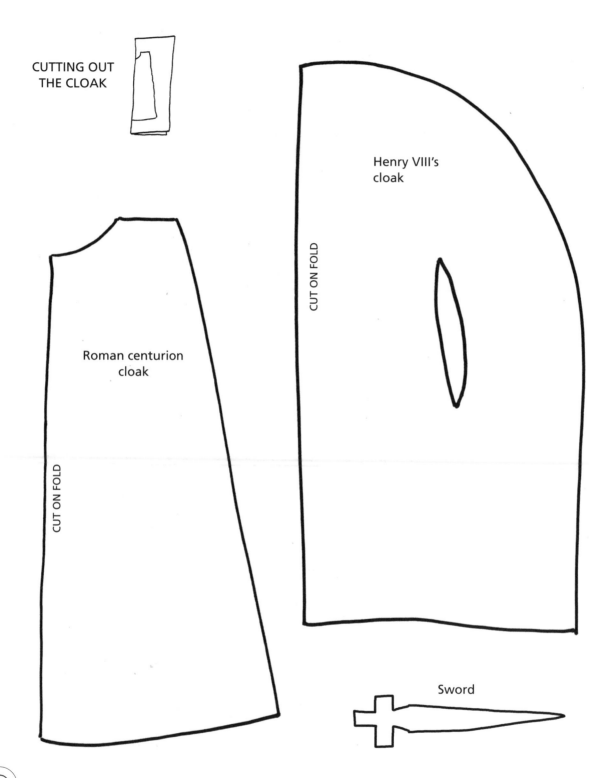

CUTTING OUT
THE CLOAK

Henry VIII's
cloak

CUT ON FOLD

Roman centurion
cloak

CUT ON FOLD

Sword

HOW TO MAKE A PAIR OF TROUSERS (BIG OR SMALL)

 Cut out two legs.

CUT OUT
2 TROUSER LEGS
FROM ANY FABRIC

 Fold each leg in half with the right side of the fabric facing in and sew a seam along the inside leg about 5mm in from the edge.

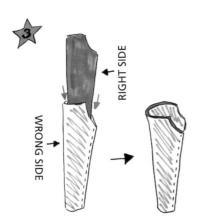

RIGHT SIDE

WRONG SIDE

Turn one leg the right way round. Put this one inside the other one so the two seams are against each other and you have the curved crotch seam in front of you.

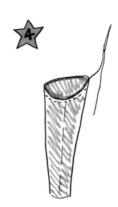 Sew the curved crotch seams together.

 Turn the trousers the right way round. Tie on with a piece of string. This is the same basic trouser construction method that every tailor uses (apart from the string bit) – so if you are feeling confident you can now make a pair of trousers for yourself!

p.98 Peg doll figures

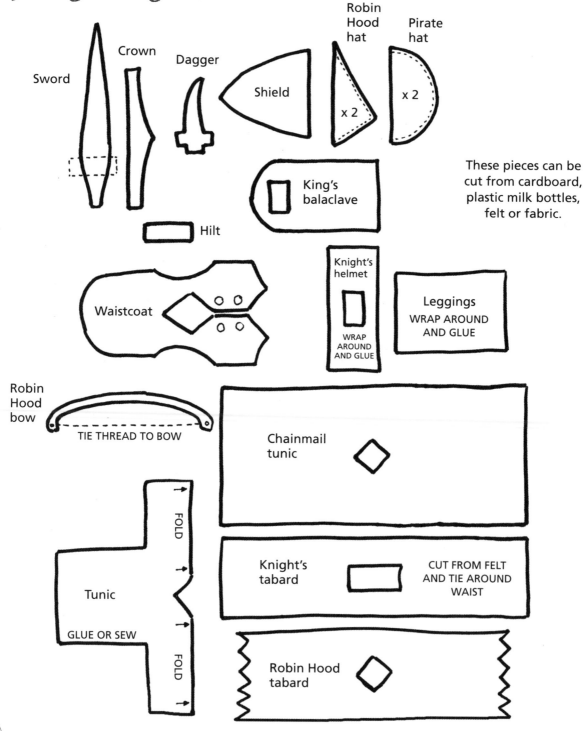

Sword

Crown

Dagger

Shield

Robin Hood hat
x 2

Pirate hat
x 2

These pieces can be cut from cardboard, plastic milk bottles, felt or fabric.

King's balaclave

Hilt

Waistcoat

Knight's helmet
WRAP AROUND AND GLUE

Leggings
WRAP AROUND AND GLUE

Robin Hood bow
TIE THREAD TO BOW

Chainmail tunic

Tunic
FOLD
FOLD
GLUE OR SEW

Knight's tabard
CUT FROM FELT AND TIE AROUND WAIST

Robin Hood tabard

p.105 Teddy angels   Enlarge or shrink to fit your teddy

Thanks

A big thank you to all the children who have inspired us with their enthusiasm, creativity and willingness to step away from the PlayStation (occasionally!)

Abe, Alfred, Alice, Asa, Bayram, Dai, Flossie, Freddie, Hal, Harry, Iris, Isaac, Joe, Kay, Laura, Linus, Louis B, Louis C, Louis M, Louis S, Martha, Max, Milo, Oliver, Seamus and Stamford